Spells for Love and Success

Spells for Love and Success

by
Jasmine Brook

Abbeydale Press

First Published in 2001 by Bookmart Limited
© 2001 Bookmart Limited

Abbeydale Press is an imprint of Bookmart Limited
Registered number 2372865
Desford Road
Enderby
Leicester
LE9 5AD

ISBN: 1861470266

Produced for Bookmart Limited by
SGA Illustration and Design
18 High Street
Hadleigh
Suffolk
IP7 5AP

Project Manager
Helen Parker (SGA)

Author
Jasmine Brook

Design
Trait Creative Solutions

Illustrator
Stephen Sweet (SGA)

PRINTED IN HONG KONG

Contents

Introduction to Magic

Magic is a powerful energy source that lies within all of us. It can be used for incredible effect if channelled correctly. When we carry out spells or rituals, we focus our minds and 'tap into' this natural source of energy. The true use of magic can enrich and transform your life.

By harnessing this powerful tool, you will be able to bring about changes that you would never have imagined possible!

Unfortunately, magic has been given a bad name over the centuries, and spell-casting is today still viewed with suspicion. Mention the word 'magic' to most people and they will instantly conjure up an image of witches on broomsticks, wearing long, pointed hats! This concept has nothing to do with true, 'white' magic, and if you are concerned that you are entering the realm of the occult – fear not!

The spells described in this book are designed only for good magic, never bad. As long as you follow the simple laws set out, your spell-casting can only improve your world and the world of those around you.

Spells for Love and Success

Love and success enthral us. We pursue them actively, but often feel they are unattainable ideals. In fact, both love and success are well within our grasp – if only we choose to overcome our fears and, instead, reach out to take hold of that which we desire.

Magic can help us to achieve our dreams by harnessing the powerful energy of thought. If we truly believe our desires will come true, they are far more likely to!

Love is a mystery – it seems so transient and when we are least looking for it, it often appears! Success sometimes seems just as mystifying – is it all down to chance, or luck? One basic law holds fast –

to find true love and happiness, we must first love and respect ourselves. Many of the spells in this book are intended to 'free' us from negative emotions and open up the path to new experiences and feelings.

Along the way, you may well find the love and success that you are looking for!

The Art of Spell Making

Most spells require 'tools of the trade'. Many are simple and can be performed with everyday objects, such as candles and essential oils. Others require more advanced equipment, including the magic wand, altar and sacred circle.

As well as using specific physical equipment, spell-casting also draws upon mental and spiritual tools. Visualisation techniques and meditations are used to give power to the spell, manifesting desires in the mind before they become a physical reality.

The spells within this book require just a few basic tools, the essential spell-casting tools are as follows.

You will need:

- Magic altar
- Magic wand
- Sacred circle
- Herbs and essential oils
- Crystals and candles

The Altar

In essence, the altar is a 'special place' before which you can meditate and create spells. Your altar can be as lavish or as simple as you like, but it is best to create it in a focal place, such as a windowsill or mantelpiece. You can place crystals, flowers, candles and other decorative objects on your altar.

The Magic Wand

The wand puts energy into a spell.
It is best made from the wood of a living
tree. Remember to ask permission before
you cut your wand.

The Sacred Circle

This is a powerful area that
symbolises perfect cosmic energy.
Spells performed within it will be
strengthened by its force. A magic
circle can be cast by marking the
area with chalk, stones or other
objects, or by circling your wand
in the air.

Preparing for True Love

To find true love,
one must be true

For then true love
will come to you!

Love is rarely found where we look for it. Sometimes, it is right before our eyes, but we can't see it! We can also look so hard for an ideal love, that we fail to recognise love in other forms. Frantically searching for love does not usually result in a happy outcome – it is far better to allow love to take its course and find you en route. Spell-casting can help to bring love your way by improving your vision of yourself. If you feel worthy of love and are truly ready for it, you can be sure that it will knock at your door.

Feelings can lurk at the end of a relationship, particularly if ended badly. Rather than giving ourselves time to come to terms with these emotions, we often look for love too soon. When we do so, we are in danger of bringing old feelings and past hurts to a new love affair. Before we can move on and commit to new relationships, these emotions must be 'cleared'.

This spell is ideal for casting out all ill-feelings and paving the way to a new beginning. It should be performed on a Friday – the day ruled by Venus, Goddess of Love.

♥ **A pink candle**

Light your candle and place it on your altar. Breathe deeply and, as you exhale, acknowledge any emotions that appear. Think through how you feel about your experiences, allowing yourself to explore any emotions. Do not rush this part of the ritual – it can often take a while to let emotions surface fully. As you release the feelings, repeat the following verse aloud:

Goddess of Love, set me free

Bring a new love soon to me

Make Way for Magic

Universal riches will always flow free

Follow their path – wherever it leads!

Most spiritual texts teach us that the Universe is a truly abundant source, in which our needs and wants will be met if only we ask. This is a theory that also holds true in magic. Magic teaches us that we can achieve our desires and live our lives in abundance – if only we unlock the key to these Universal riches in our minds.

Too often people view 'abundance' as a source of never-ending wealth. 'Abundance' in the magical sense means to have all that you truly need for fulfilment and happiness. Universal abundance is a term that describes the flow of positive energy and prosperity. The belief in its existence opens up a channel to this energy. By using the power of visualisation and positive thought, we can imagine ourselves completely fulfilled and in doing so manifest this image as a reality in our lives.

Like spells for love, spells for prosperity also require a 'cleansing' or 'clearing' of all negative thoughts. If we harbour a belief that we will never attain success or that which we need, the thought energy we send out may actually manifest these ideas. To attract prosperity, perform this simple ritual on a Thursday evening and riches will soon start to flow your way!

You will need:

- A green candle
- Incense
- Paper and a pen

Light your candle and place it on your altar. Scatter a few drops of incense about the candle, then write a list of your worst financial fears. Close your eyes and think of the most awful thing that might happen to you.

Let yourself feel this fear completely, then release it from your body by repeating the incantation.

Fear, I command thee to fly forth
Release me to find a freer course

Letting Go of Love

A heart freed from grief and sorrow

Will find true love on the 'morrow

People often hang on to their past disappointments and failed love affairs, while this very action may well prevent them from finding the perfect love they so crave! There is a certain truth in the belief that relationships formed on the 'rebound' are not usually successful, unless both parties have overcome feelings from the past.

To let go of past loves and hurts, perform this ritual on a Friday evening, as the moon is waning. It should be carried out within your sacred circle.

You will need:

- ♥ A pink candle
- ♥ Incense
- ♥ Paper and coloured pens

Light your candle and sit peacefully within your circle. Scatter a few drops of incense about the candle, then write down any past loves and hurts that come to mind. As you list each memory, mark a colour next to it – whichever appears in your thoughts. When you have given a colour to each memory, write next to it the emotions that you associate with the written words and colours. Be completely honest with yourself as you write – remember, this list is for your eyes only!

When completed, read the list aloud. As you do so, imagine the words and feelings are released out of your body into the Universe and transformed into light!

Keep the paper close to you for a further three days and nights. On Monday evening, repeat the ritual with the following incantation:

From this day forth,
my heart will be free
To find love and
happiness, eternally

The Magic in All of Us

The power of magic lies within us all

We must listen to hear its call

The Universe is full of abundance – we need only search for it and it will come our way. However, if we create obstacles in our own minds and believe that we are not deserving or worthy of luck or fortune, we prevent ourselves from attaining the very thing we seek. Magic can help to open up the channels – by allowing yourself to visualise your life becoming filled with riches, you start upon the path to achieving them.

Perform this spell to make possible and bring true all of your dreams!

You will need:

- A pen
- Paper
- A green candle
- Mint oil
- Incense

Add a few drops of mint essential oil to your candle and decorate your altar with symbols of abundance, such as jewellery, green crystals and photos of friends or loved ones.

Carve your name three times in the wax of your candle, once on the front and once on each side. Light the candle and place it on your altar.

On your paper, draw a picture of your perfect life – filled with prosperity.

Place this on your altar for three days and nights. Light your candle and incense every day. To complete the ritual, repeat the incantation aloud each night as you go to sleep.

Goddess Moon,
show me the way
To a new beginning
with the dawn of day

Bring Me Love

Seek true love with
an open heart

For then it will surely
cross your path

A perfect romance is possible! It does
not always take the form that you had
imagined, however, nor does it usually
appear when you expect it. Love cannot
be forced, but should instead be
encouraged to grow and develop in
its own time.

If you are in search of a perfect partner,
simply lure them in with your magical
powers! Perform this simple spell on a
Friday night, then sit back and wait for
true love to take its course – wherever it
may lead!

You will need:

♥ Pink candles

♥ Patchouli and sandalwood oils

♥ Paper and coloured pens

Choose two pink candles, and anoint
them with patchouli and sandalwood
essential oils. Mark your initials in
the wax and place the candles on your
altar. Draw representations of the four
elements (air, water, wind and fire) and
place one on each corner of your altar.

Draw a picture of your heart and write
down the qualities that you look for in
a lover. Note their age, appearance and
emotional disposition – take care to
write down all of the details that are
important to you.

The fuller a picture you create now, the more power your spell will have. As you visualise your ideal partner, repeat aloud the incantation to Goddess Love.

Goddess Love
my heart seeks another
Pray send me soon
my perfect lover

Wreathed in Success

The scent of a single flower

Can lend your plans a magical power

Flowers have many magical properties, and different plants can be used to enhance your spells. The scent and colour of flowers can evoke powerful thoughts and will increase the effectiveness of any ritual. The flowers used in this spell are known to attract success and prosperity – may they bring you luck!

You can select any or all of the flowers listed. They work equally well on their own, or combined within the wreath.

You will need:

- A small willow wand

  or
- A wreathing circle from a flower shop
- Clematis, jasmine or peony flowers
- Green embroidery thread
- A green candle
- Lemon balm oil

Anoint your candle with a few drops of the lemon balm oil, then place it on your altar and light. Select the flowers that you wish to use for the wreath and lay them before the altar.

As you breathe in the scent from the burning oil, repeat the incantation.

Then carefully weave your chosen flowers into a wreath. If you are using a willow wand, gently bend the wand into a circle and secure with some strong twine. Tie the flowers to the wreathing circle with the green embroidery thread, securing them just below the flower head. Once your wreath is decorated with the flowers, sit quietly for a few moments and imagine your life becoming rich with success and prosperity. Place the wreath inside your home, at a focal point you often pass or look at. Every time you look at the wreath, imagine your success coming to fruition!

Fortune
and prosperity
Bring your
riches unto me
Let this spell
empower my work
May it harness
the treasure of
the Earth

Beauty is in the Eye of the Spell-caster!

Scent and magic walk hand-in-hand

Let them lead you to a beautiful land!

As any spell-caster knows, scent can be used for powerful effect, and never more so than when used in spells for love. 'Bathing beauties' can attract the love and romance of their dreams by performing this simple spell! The ritual should be carried out on a Monday – the day of feminine qualities.

The oils that you use should be selected for the desired result – to attract romance use jasmine and rose, for passion, basil, neroli and ylang-ylang.

You will need:

- Two pink candles
- Neroli, ylang-ylang and basil oils

  or

- Jasmine and rose oils

Collect your materials and take them to your bathroom. Anoint the candles with a few drops of your chosen oils and place them in a safe position within the room. Light the candles and allow the scent to fill the air.

Run yourself a hot bath, adding a few drops of the oils you have selected to the water. The oils will disperse in the water, filling the room with their aroma and intoxicating your senses.

As you bathe, look into the candlelight and imagine whatever you wish for coming to fruition. If you seek romantic love, visualise yourself bewitching your dream lover with your feminine charms. If you wish to add passion to your life, visualise yourself as a beautiful and bewitching goddess! As you imagine your desires, repeat the following:

Venus, may my dreams become true
Let love and passion my life renew

Crystal Magic

Within each crystal is a magical force

Let it lead you to a truer course

Crystals carry mysterious power and can enhance any spell that you cast. They are extremely beneficial in meditation. Crystals are used for various purposes in spell-casting, depending on their type and colour. They can be used in simple meditation exercises, or for more complicated sachet or placket spells. Their powers are such that they are also often used on their own as healing or proctective charms. This spell uses their properties to attract success.

You will need:

- Two green crystals
- Two gold candles
- Mint essential oil

Place the two candles on your altar and anoint them with some of the mint oil. Light the candles and breathe in the scent from the oil.

Hold the two crystals at eye level, before the candle flames. Gaze deeply into their colour and allow yourself to become entranced by their appearance.

Fixing your sight upon the crystals, meditate upon your plan or venture. Imagine yourself successful and all your hopes coming to fruition. Confirm your success in your mind with the affirmation to Goddess Earth.

When you are fully convinced of your powers, blow out the candles. Make sure you keep the crystals in your pockets or on your person as you go about your plans – they will help to reaffirm your intentions.

Goddess Earth, fill me with your force

Help me to chart a fruitful course

A Spell for Prosperity

Universal riches are within your grasp

To make them yours, simply ask!

In keeping with Universal law, this spell requires that you first give something of yourself in order that you will receive in return. To draw prosperity in, carry out the following ritual on a Sunday, during a new moon.

On the Sunday before you perform the ritual, put the gold coin in a pocket of your clothing and carry it with you for the following seven days. Within that time, perform a task for another that requires something of yourself in both time and energy.

You will need:

- A gold coin
- A gold candle
- A pinch of allspice
- A square of orange material
- A length of orange cord
- A green crystal

The following Sunday evening, sit within your sacred circle and place a pinch of allspice in all four directions: North, East, South and West. Light your candle and in front of (but not through) the flame make a circle with the coin seven times. As you do so, repeat the incantation.

On the seventh circle place the coin and the green crystal inside the orange material and tie together with the orange cord. Carry this with you.

Universal power, help
me to understand

The perfection of
your wondrous plan

By giving to others,
I will receive

Everything I desire
and truly need

Finally, gather up all four pinches of
allspice. As you pick up each pinch, hold
it tightly in your hand and visualise your
spell coming to fruition.

Bury the spice at the base of a tree and
give thanks as you do so. Your spell is
complete – may future prosperity be yours!

Bring Passion to Your Life

Let passions glow
relight your fire

With this spell
manifest your desire!

You will need:

- A red candle
- Two or three violet flowers
- A base oil
- Ylang-ylang oil

Violets have long been used as a powerful love potion – both the ancient Greeks and Romans swore by them as passion providers! If your relationship is lacking passion, try this spell to bring the excitement back.

On opposite sides of the candle, carve both your name and your lover's. Entwine the letters so that they encircle the candle. Place it on your altar and scent it with a few drops of ylang-ylang oil. Carefully pluck the petals from your violets and place them around the candle.

Pour some base oil into the palm of your hand, add a few drops of ylang-ylang oil and some of the violet petals. Hold the oil up to your face and breathe in its scent. As you do so, imagine your relationship refilled with passion. Repeat aloud the incantation.

Place the passion-packed oil in an incense burner and light it. Let its scent set your lover on fire.

Let nature's power
rekindle our flame

Inspire our hearts
with passion again!

Fortune Hunting!

Luck and prosperity will abound

If good fortune is truly found

It is generally assumed that good luck is something that befalls you by chance, and that there is nothing you can do to bring it your way. This is not so – for spell-casting can help to bring you luck and fortune! If you feel the need to improve your fortunes, perform this spell under an oak tree on a Thursday evening, during a full moon.

You will need to make a spell-bag on the Thursday a week before you perform the spell. Spell-bags are quite simple to make, as follows:

For the bag you will need:

- A square of gold silk
- A length of gold cord
- Sequin stars and moons
- A needle and thread

Carefully cut 6-8 small holes around the four sides of the silk square, about 1 cm from the edge. These should be big enough to pass the gold cord through. Thread the gold cord through the holes and draw together to make a pouch. Decorate your bag with sequin stars and moons.

Beneath the oak tree, anoint the crystal and ribbon with some of the oil. As you do so, imagine that you are lifted up by the strength of the oak trees' branches.

For the spell you will need:

- A piece of gold ribbon
- Nutmeg oil
- A sprig of honeysuckle
- The spell-bag
- A blue crystal

Place the crystal, ribbon and honeysuckle inside the spell-bag and offer it up to the oak tree. Repeat aloud the incantation.

Whenever you wish to bring yourself luck, carry your spell-bag. It will help to empower any venture that you undertake.

Jupiter, let good
fortune ride with me
Like the oak tree, may
it lift me up
And fill my life with
hope and luck

Bewitch a Lover

Empower yourself with a special charm

To bring a lover into your arms!

You will need:

- A locket
- Neroli oil
- Herbs: lavender, basil and dill
- A length of gold cord

The talisman is a powerful piece of jewellery. It is known to attract positive energy and has been used for as long as anyone can remember to attract love. Talismans can also take on properties, depending on the reason for their use. They can be designed as powerful magnets to attract abundance and prosperity. Likewise, they can be used as a channel to attract and hold love. To bewitch your intended lover, perform this spell on a Tuesday evening, as the moon appears.

Scent the locket with some drops of oil. Cut a few nail clippings and a few tips from the ends of your hair. Place both inside the locket with the herbs, and seal it.

Attach the gold cord to the locket to make a pendant, and hold it towards the sky. Imagine yourself as a bewitching and enchanting goddess!

As you do so, repeat the incantation aloud three times.

Magic talisman,
my secret treasure

Intoxicate my lover,
now and forever!

Winds of Change

With the winds of
change may you see

How wondrous life
can truly be!

- **Two purple candles**
- **Marjoram, ginger and mimosa oils**
- **Blue paper and a pen**

We are naturally frightened of change. We feel stable and secure if our lives follow the same pattern, and the thought of disruption and alteration can seem unnerving. Change, however, can often be good. It can shake us from a mediocre existence and bring about extraordinary events. If you feel that your life is in need of change, perform this ritual on a Monday night during a waxing moon.

Anoint your candles with the essential oils and place them on your altar.

Breathe deeply and allow your mind to relax. On a piece of blue paper, write down how you would like your life to change. Allow whichever thoughts come into your mind to work their way onto your list – do not hold back.

Keep the list close to you for the following week. The next Monday evening, relight your candles and open up the list. Read the words aloud again and mentally affirm your desire for change.

When you have finished, hold
out the paper in front of you
and repeat this incantation
five times:

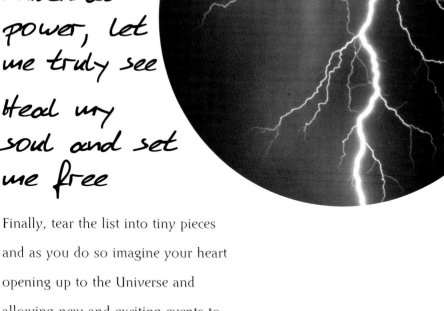

Universal
power, let
me truly see
Heal my
soul and set
me free

Finally, tear the list into tiny pieces
and as you do so imagine your heart
opening up to the Universe and
allowing new and exciting events to
enter. Feel yourself open to change...
however unexpected the results!

The Magic of Scent

*If a lady's heart
you wish to win*

*With scented magic,
invite love in!*

Men can also use the power of
spell-casting to improve their love life!
If you find yourself admiring a lady
from afar, or would like to put some
much-needed zest back into your love
life, try out this spell.

This spell takes a leaf out of the book of
traditional courtship – you must woo
the lady you wish to win! Plan to change
your normal routine and surprise her
with something special – it could be a
present, a surprise meal or even a
weekend away.

You will need:

- A base oil
- Lemon, ylang-ylang
  and neroli oils
- An incense burner

Before your romantic occasion, pour
some base oil into your burner and add
a few drops of each essential oil. Light
your burner and repeat the chant.

As the scent of the oil flows over you,
imagine yourself winning over your
lover with romance.

38

Magical scent,
fulfil my desires

Set my lover's
heart on fire!

Something Special

Something special can be yours

Simply follow these Universal laws

You will need:

- Green crystals
- A small orange candle
- Bergamot and peony oils
- A small pot

If you wish for something special, all you have to do is ask! Perform this ritual on a Thursday evening, during a waxing moon, and your desires may soon be winging your way!

Create a circle on your altar with the crystals. On one side of the candle carve your name, on the other draw whatever you desire! Anoint the candle with two or three drops of bergamot oil, and light it. Place the candle in the centre of your magical circle. Leave it unlit for eight days and seven nights.

On the eighth night, place a few drops of peony oil on the candle, light it and meditate upon your picture. Conjure up an image of what it is that you truly desire – imagine it coming true.
Allow the candle to burn right down, then take the wax and place it in a pot whilst repeating the chant.

Finally, bury the pot in your garden. Continue to meditate upon whatever it is you wish for – remember, the Universe has a way of presenting our desires when we least expect it!

Goddess Earth,
take this spell

A seed I cast
into your well

My secret wish,
pray bring to me
This, Goddess Earth,
I ask of thee

Love Child!

If passion is lacking in your life

This spell will soon its fire relight!

For a relationship that has lost the passion of youth, this spell can help to restore forgotten ardour! It is also a powerful fertility ritual, so don't be surprised if your spell-casting brings more than you had bargained for! Perform the spell on a Monday evening.

Place the candles around the bedroom and anoint with some ylang-ylang oil. (Make sure not to place the candles near anything flammable.) Pour the rest of the oil into your perfume dispenser and spray your sheets and the air.

You will need:

- Three to five green candles
- A perfume spray dispenser
- Ylang-ylang oil

As you light the candles, repeat the incantation to Goddess Diana.

Old folklore claims that the oak tree is a powerful fertility aid. If you want to enhance fertility, carry an acorn with you, or place one under your pillow!

Goddess Diana,
grant me my wish
Renew my life with
a lover's kiss!

New Horizons

Lady Luck carry me home

On land or sea may I safely roam

Travellers have used good luck charms and symbols for protection since early times. Traditionally, medallions bearing the image of St Christopher (the patron saint of travellers) have been worn, but there are many older symbols and icons which can also help protect from harm.

If you have plans for travel, or are about to venture into business abroad, try out this spell on a Wednesday evening to bring good fortune to your venture.

You will need:

- A yellow candle
- Orange oil
- Green paper
- Some fennel herb
- A pen

Place a pinch of the fennel herb at the four points of your sacred circle: North, East, South and West. Sit inside the circle and anoint your candle with some drops of the oil.

Facing East, draw a large triangle on your piece of paper – the triangle is a known symbol for air.

Hold the paper before you and repeat the incantation.

Elements of the
air watch over me

Carry me safely
on land or sea

Guide me along
my journey's path

Hold me firm,
hold me fast

Fold up your piece of paper and keep
it with you on your journey or
venture. Remember to bury the fennel
herb you used somewhere safe before
you leave.

Sweet as Honey

*A bitter heart will
only burn
True love will make
the sweetness return*

This verse is very true – harbouring ill feelings and grudges does not make for a happy and long-lasting relationship. It is far better to put bad feelings aside and start again – and a little bit of magic may help you along the way!

If your relationship has been soured with arguments and bitter quarrels, put the sweetness back into it with this gentle spell!

Embroider your name on one ribbon and your partner's on the other. Tie the ribbons together in a knot and put them

You will need:

- A small jam-jar
- A spoonful of honey
- Two pink ribbons
- Light blue embroidery thread and a needle
- A pink rose bush

in the jam-jar. Pour a spoonful of honey over the ribbons and cover with the lid.

Ideally the next part of this ritual should be performed with your lover, but you can carry it out on your own if you wish. In your garden, or a piece of land that you can use, dig a hole for the rose. Before you plant it, place the jam-jar inside the hole, then plant the rose. As you do so, repeat the incantation to Goddess Earth.

Carefully look after your rose and each year cut a few blooms to place on your altar – it will help to keep your relationship as sweet as honey!

Goddess Earth, let the sweetness of life

Silently cease our quarrels and strife!

Draw My Love to Me!

To find love within another's eyes

Simply look towards the skies!

Love plackets are simple but highly effective instruments for drawing in sensual love. Inside the placket you can place symbols or objects that will enhance your spell. If you would like to attract romantic love, or spice up your love life, try out this ritual. Perform it in the evening on a Tuesday – the day ruled by Mars, God of Lust!

To make your placket, cut the two squares of material (20 cm long by 20 cm wide) and place on top of each other. Sew the two squares together along three edges,

You will need:

- Two squares of red silk
- Red thread and a needle
- A picture of the planet Mars
- Ylang-ylang oil
- A red crystal
- A small snip of your hair
- A red candle

leaving the top edge open. Turn the placket inside out so that the sewn edges are hidden.

Place your picture of Mars, the red crystal and the small snip of your hair inside the placket. Place the placket on your altar.

Anoint the candle with a few drops of ylang-ylang oil, and light it. As you look at the glowing candlelight, imagine

yourself intoxicated by
passionate love! Once you
have fully meditated upon
your wish, stand back
from the altar.

Leave the placket on the
altar for a full 21 days
without disturbing it.

Remember – you can only aim to
attract passion into your life. You
cannot force another into something
against their will. If you use magic for
this purpose it will only rebound upon
you thrice-fold!

Lady Luck, Bring Me Luck!

Faith and fortune will never part

You'll find both in a trusting heart

Just as plackets can be used to bring you love, they can also be used to attract luck and success. As with all spells for prosperity and success, the first step to achieving your goal is to imagine yourself as already successful. The ritual of making a placket and devoting yourself to the task will help to reinforce your intention. The placket will be empowered with a magical force and will continue to generate the positive energy instilled within it during spell-casting. To bring good fortune your way, perform this ritual on a Sunday evening.

You will need:

- Two squares of green silk
- Green thread and a needle
- Orange oil
- An orange crystal
- A green candle
- A photograph of yourself

Make your luck placket by sewing the two squares of green silk together (they should be roughly 20 cm long by 20 cm wide). Remember to sew just three edges, leaving the top edge open. Turn inside out to conceal the seams.

Inside the placket, place the photograph of yourself. Anoint your crystal with a few drops of orange oil, and also place this inside. Carefully lay your luck placket on the altar.

Anoint your candle with a few drops of the orange oil, place it next to the placket on the altar and light it. Concentrating upon the glowing light of the candle, allow yourself to imagine your life filled with luck and fortune. As you do so, repeat the following incantation:

Hear my wish,
Goddess Earth

Let good luck
find my path

Bring fortune
to my life

Grant me this
wish I ask

Romance Blossoms!

If love is grown with tender care

Its fruitful flower you will ever share!

Flowers are a symbol of love and have long been used by lovers to woo another. Flowers can also be used in love spell-casting to enhance, attract or renew love. The properties of rose oil are known to be a powerful aid when seeking love, and it is no secret that the rose is the most commonly given flower during a love affair. It symbolises love itself. The rose is the most well-known of all romantic flowers, but there are a number of other flowers which can also be used to enhance love.

You will need:

- Pansy, poppy, tulip and violet seeds or bulbs
- Thyme seeds
- A window-box
- Planting soil
- A pink candle
- Rose oil

If you would like to encourage a new relationship, try out this spell to bring it into full bloom!

Anoint your candle with a few drops of rose oil and place it on your altar. Before the altar, fill your window-box with planting soil and plant the flower and herb seeds or bulbs. As you do so, imagine you are firmly rooting the seeds of your relationship in fertile soil and repeat aloud the incantation.

Water the soil and place the full window-box in a window.

Each day, tend the window-box and watch the flowers and herbs grow. As you care for the plants, imagine that you are caring for your relationship and nurturing it into full bloom. With all this care and attention, what love could fail to blossom!

Goddess of Love,
like the seeds I sow
Let my love blossom
and grow

Fortune, Ride with Me!

It may be an uncharted road

That leads the way towards your goal

Talismans have been worn by people since ancient times to attract luck and fortune. Made on the appropriate days of the week, talismans help to create powerful thought energies that can attract your desires. A good luck talisman should be made on a Sunday – the day of fortune and hope.

Make your talisman from materials appropriate for your spell. Good luck talismans should be made from gold, the material that represents the sun god Ra, god of wealth and luck.

Carefully pluck 2-3 petals from the marigold flower. Lay the petals on your altar and anoint them with a few drops of the orange oil. Lay the golden locket before the altar.

Place your candle on the altar and anoint it with a few drops of orange oil. As you light it, repeat the incantation.

Carefully place the marigold petals inside the locket and seal. Wear your talisman until you feel you have attracted whatever fortune you are seeking. When you have fulfilled your wishes, bury the talisman in the ground.

Gods of Fortune,
ride with me

Bring me luck
and prosperity

Make Love, Not War

Cease all quarrels and all strife

Let love add stillness to your life!

This spell will help to heal a relationship after a quarrel or separation. Ideally, it should be performed with the partner, or lover with whom you have quarrelled. However, you can perform it on your own if the partner proves to be reluctant!

This ritual is very simple, but highly effective. The act of tying two knots in the pink ribbon will help to seal a relationship and draw lovers close once more. By leaving the ribbon before the altar, the energy created during the

You will need:

- Two pink candles
- An incense burner
- A base oil
- Sandalwood oil
- A few coriander seeds
- A pink ribbon

spell-casting will continue to flow and heal any rift in the relationship.

Place the two candles on your altar and anoint them with a few drops of sandalwood oil. Light the candles.

Pour a small amount of the base oil into your incense burner, then add some drops of sandalwood oil. Light the burner and allow the incense to scent the air.

Drop your coriander seeds into the oil mixture. As the scent rises from the burner, tie two knots in your pink ribbon and repeat the chant.

Place the ribbon before the altar and leave it there for 21 days. Each day, meditate upon your spell, touching the ribbon to let its positive energy flow through you.

Venus, Goddess of Love
Let our troubles soon vanish
Bind us together once more
This is our sincere wish

A Spell for a Successful Career

Let your thoughts carry you through

Look for luck and it will find you!

You will need:

- A blue candle
- Sandalwood oil
- Four blue crystals
- A golden tin or box

Interviews can strike terror into anyone! Don't let nerves get the better of you, employ some simple rituals to make your career moves carefree. If you are about to attend an interview, the following spell will help to ensure that it all runs smoothly.

On the evening before your interview, carve your name into one side of the candle and anoint it with a few drops of sandalwood oil. Place the four crystals at each point of your sacred circle, then put the candle within the circle and light it.

Watch the candle as it burns. The colour of the candle will help you to visualise your success – blue is the colour for thought and communication. Imagine yourself full of confidence and success. Repeat the incantation.

When the candle has burnt down, pick up the crystals and place them inside a golden tin or box within your home. If you don't have a box, you can use gold wrapping paper to wrap the crystals up.

During your interview, try to concentrate on transmitting positive thoughts. Imagine yourself sending out a channel of warmth and positive energy.

Now that you've opened up the pathways of communication, you can relax! What will be, will be.

Universal power,
fill me with your
mighty force

Let me find
success, whatever
be my course

Love by Candlelight

Candlelight can lead to enrapture –

An enchanted heart is easy to capture!

If you are planning a romantic evening with your lover, a simple spell or ritual beforehand will add a touch of magic to the occasion! Certain candles and oils will create a special atmosphere and will help to intoxicate whoever is in the room!

As with all spells, select the candle colour and oils for the intended purpose of the ritual. If you wish to add romance to your evening, use pink candles and the oils listed for love. If passion is your passion, use red candles and the appropriate oils!

You will need:

- Four to six red or pink candles
- For love: gardenia, jasmine, lavender and rose oils
- For passion: basil, cinnamon, ginger, neroli or ylang-ylang oils

Before the evening commences, place the candles in front of your altar. Select just two of the oils suggested for passion or love and anoint the candles with a few drops of the oil. Light the candles and breathe in their scent. As you do so, meditate upon your wishes and desires for the occasion. Imagine whatever you visualise coming true – see it in your mind. Affirm your thoughts by repeating aloud the chant.

When you have a firm and positive image in your mind, blow out the candles and place them in the room in which you will be entertaining. Place the candles around the room so that their light will surround you and your lover. Re-light the candles and allow the scent of the oils to fill the air before your guest arrives.

Throughout the evening, reconfirm your thoughts and repeat the incantation silently. May it all go as you have planned!

Let this love by
candlelight
Fill my thoughts,
day and night

Healing a Broken Heart

*A heart that feels
both hurt and pain*

*Will one day feel
true love again!*

For a heart broken in love, spell-casting can help to heal disappointment and upset. You can use this spell to help mend the heart of another, or your own. If performing for another, replace the lock of your hair with a lock from the person you are helping, and the gift with one of their own. Carry out this spell on a Sunday evening.

To make a placket, place the two pieces of material together (they should be roughly 20 cm long by 20 cm wide) and sew along three of the edges.

You will need:

- Two pieces of light blue material
- Blue thread and a needle
- A blue candle
- Rosemary oil
- A green crystal
- A small gift from your lover
- A lock of your hair

Leave the top edge open and turn the placket inside out.

Anoint the crystal with a few drops of the rosemary oil, and then place it inside the placket along with the gift and the lock of hair. Add a few drops of rosemary oil to the candle, and light it. Place the candle and the placket on your altar.

Meditate upon the blue
candle and feel your
heart filling with
healing power.
Affirm in your
mind that you
are worthy of
true love and that
you deserve happiness.
Allow the candle to burn right
down as you sit quietly before it.

Leave the placket on your altar until you
feel that your heart has healed.

Planting for Fortune

Sow with the seeds of success

And your life will truly be blessed!

Herbs can be extremely potent and have been used in spell-casting since early times. The ancient Egyptians relied on many herbs to enhance their rituals, particularly mandrake, which was used to attract power, wealth, money and love.

Modern-day spell-casting uses a number of herbs to attract wealth and success. To encourage wealth your way, carry out this ritual on a Thursday evening. Allow the aromas in this spell to fill the air and breathe in the heady scents.

You will need:

- A green candle
- A small jam-jar
- A base oil
- A pinch of ginger
- A pinch of allspice
- Nutmeg and pine oils
- A honeysuckle bush

Before your altar, anoint the candle with a few drops of nutmeg and pine essential oils, then light. Place a small amount of the base oil in the jam-jar and into this mix a few drops of the essential oils.

Add a pinch of ginger and allspice to the oil mixture. Screw on the lid, and shake thoroughly. Place the jar next to the candle and repeat the incantation to Mother Earth.

Blow out the candle and take the jar and honeysuckle bush into your garden, or a place where you may plant it.

Before planting the honeysuckle, sprinkle the ground with your oil mixture. Repeat the incantation again, and then plant the bush.

As the bush grows, meditate upon your desires – imagine wealth and abundance growing alongside it. May it flow your way!

Mother Earth, I
offer you this gift
May its fruits
fulfill my wish

Love Letters to Win Another!

A spell made with unfounded cause

Will return to the caster, with force

A note of warning precedes this spell – true spell-casters never attempt to bend the will of another or create spells with intended harm. One should never try to win away someone else's lover, and according to the laws of nature, all spells cast will eventually be revisited upon the caster!

However, sometimes love needs a helping hand. If your intentions are true, this spell should help to swiftly bring the object of your desires to your side!

You will need:

- An ink pen
- Red ink
- A sheet of writing paper
- An envelope
- A pink candle
- Lavender and jasmine oils
- A marigold flower

Anoint your candle with some drops of lavender oil and light it. Place it on your altar. Take the sheet of paper and write a love letter to your intended, in red ink. Red is the colour of sensual passion and will help to transmit your desires. Write whatever comes to mind – it can be a poem, a song or a simple letter.

When your letter is complete, hold it before the candlelight and read it aloud. Affirm the message to your intended and imagine you are sending out thoughts in a wave of light, straight towards their heart!

Scent the paper with jasmine oil, put the marigold flower on the letter and place it inside the envelope, but do not seal it. Put the letter on your altar and leave it there for 21 days. Each day, read the letter aloud before your altar – may your love be reciprocated!

Marvellous Magic!

Fortunes can be made and found

Upon the Earth's fruitful ground

This spell is designed for those seeking to increase their profits in business, or about to enter into a take-over bid. If you want to bring wealth your way and ensure success in your venture, perform this ritual on a Thursday evening, under a waxing moon.

Begin your spell by anointing all eight candles with some almond oil before your altar. Do not light them yet. Scent the orange scarf with a few drops of the mint essential oil and tie it loosely around your neck.

You will need:

- Eight silver coins
- Eight green candles
- A handful of almond nuts
- An orange scarf
- Almond and mint oils
- A basket

Place the eight silver coins in one pocket, and the handful of almond nuts in the other. Put your candles in the basket and carefully carry them outside into your garden, or a quiet place where you will not be disturbed. This spell requires a peaceful environment in order to allow you to visualise your desires.

Under the moonlight, place the eight silver coins in a circle. Make sure that the head of each coin is facing upwards.

Place a candle on each coin, until you have a complete circle of standing candles. Light the candles and repeat aloud the spell to Goddess Moon.

As you say the spell aloud, imagine your wealth increasing beyond your wildest dreams!

Goddess Moon, as your riches unfold

Let this treasure grow ten-fold

A Spell to Hold a Lover Fast!

With this spell may your lover

Have eyes for you and no other!

If you are concerned that your lover might be about to stray, this love spell will help to put a swift end to any wandering eyes! Use it to intoxicate your lover once more and bind them firmly to your side. Carry out the ritual on a Friday evening.

Anoint your candle with a few drops of jasmine oil and place it on your altar. Put the piece of amber in front of the candle, directly before you. Sit facing the altar and inhale the scent of the jasmine as it perfumes the air.

You will need:

- One sprig of clover
- A piece of amber
- A photo of your lover
- A pink candle
- Jasmine oil

Take the photograph of your lover and hold it in one hand. In the other, clasp the sprig of clover. Breathe in the scent of the jasmine, until you feel completely calm and tranquil. As your breathing slows and your mind becomes clear, gaze upon the colour of the amber in the candlelight and imagine your loved one firmly bound to you in everlasting love and devotion. To reinforce these thoughts, repeat aloud the incantation.

Meditate upon your thoughts in front
of the candlelight – feel their
power fill the room. Leave
the photograph, amber
and clover on the altar
for fourteen days and
nights, returning to the
altar to repeat the ritual
if you feel doubts
entering again.

Venus, Goddess
of Love
Bind my lover
close to me
Let our love
soon blossom
And entwine
us eternally

Lucky Charm!

Hang a lucky charm above your door

Within you'll find luck forever more!

Spell-sachets have long been used as powerful charms. They can empower your spells and help to repel negative energies. If placed above a doorway, they can act as a protective charm for the home. If carried about your person, they will help to protect you from bad luck and misfortune. If you would like to attract good luck and success for yourself or for another, try out this spell.

Perform the spell on a Thursday evening to ensure its effectiveness. Before your altar, anoint one candle with a few drops

You will need:

- A piece of orange cloth
- A length of green cord or string
- A green crystal
- Two orange candles
- Orange and ginger oils
- A pinch of allspice

of orange oil, and the other with a few drops of ginger. Light both candles and allow the scent to infuse the air.

Lay your piece of cloth on the altar and put a pinch of allspice at its centre. Place the crystal on top and gather up all four corners to form a sachet. Tie together with the length of green cord or string. You will need to make eight knots. With each knot you make, repeat the incantation aloud to Goddess Earth.

When you have made the eighth knot, and repeated the incantation for the eighth time, lay the sachet on your altar and blow out the candles. The sachet should remain on your altar for eight days and nights to become fully empowered.

Goddess Earth,
empower this charm
Protect its holder
from any harm
May good fortune
walk their path
May good luck rest
on their hearth

Hurt by Love

Love and resentment
never rest together

Banish ill-feelings,
now and forever

You will need:

- Four pink candles
- Two green crystals
- Rosemary or sandalwood oil
- Some marjoram herb

An upset or hurt in love can cloud a relationship. Just as we often carry over feelings and hurts from past relationships into new ones, misunderstandings and harboured ill-feelings can sour existing relations. If you find it difficult to forgive a disappointment, or move on after a quarrel, this spell may help to heal the wound.

Create your sacred circle by casting it in the air with your wand, or marking it on the ground with some chalk.

At the four points of the circle, North, South, East and West, place a candle. Anoint each candle with a few drops of your chosen oil and light them. Before each candle, place a pinch of the marjoram herb.

Sit quietly at the centre of your circle and place a crystal in the palm of each hand. Holding the crystals tightly, close your eyes and imagine the feelings that you harbour within you. Envisage them as heavy weights that rest upon your shoulders restricting you.

When you are comfortable with this image, start to visualise the weights becoming lighter and transforming into feathers that float away with the wind. Imagine yourself light and free, with the emotions completely removed. As you do so, repeat aloud the chant.

Blow out the candles and throw the pinches of marjoram from a window. See them carried away in the air, like the feathers you imagined. You should now feel as light as a feather yourself!

Goddess Venus,
banish all blame
Let love walk
lightly once again

The Magic of Love

Let love enfold you
in its arms

Enrich your life with
its charms!

Love has magical properties of its own –
it seems to appear when you least expect
it, and in the strangest of places! Like
the plants and flowers all around us,
love can also blossom and grow year
after year. All it needs is some tender,
loving care! To help keep the magic of
your love alive, follow this ritual on a
Tuesday evening.

Before your altar, anoint the two candles
with some rose oil and light them. Hold
one gift in each hand before the candlelight, and repeat aloud the incantation.

You will need:

- Two daffodil bulbs
- Rose oil
- Two pink candles
- A small gift you gave your lover
- A small gift that your lover gave
  to you
- Some lavender or dill herb
- A square of white material
- A length of pink cord

Place your gifts in the centre of the
material, then put a pinch of lavender or
dill on top. Draw up all four corners of
the material to form a pouch, and tie
firmly with the pink cord. Blow out the
candles and take the sachet outside, with
your daffodil bulbs.

Find a quiet, sunny spot in your garden (or a piece of land that you can use) and dig a hole for the daffodil bulbs. Place the sachet in the hole and plant the bulbs on top.

Each year as your flowers bloom, imagine your love growing stronger and stronger, filling your life with colour and beauty.

May the magic of your love last forever!

Goddess of Love,
please bring us
eternal delight

Let our love
blossom and grow
throughout our lives

The Magic of Change

Look deep into the well of change

For there your life will begin again

You will need:

- A purple candle
- Basil oil
- A silver locket
- Some marjoram herb

Very few lives are untouched by misfortune. As any successful businessman or woman will know, success does not always flow smoothly! Magic teaches us that change can be good, it can clear out 'old rubbish' and let us start our lives again. This is often when we find the proverbial 'silver lining' in our misfortune.

If life has dealt you a blow, or thrown you off course, try out this ritual. Performed on a Saturday evening, it may help you find your silver lining!

Place a pinch of marjoram at each point of your sacred circle, North, South, East and West. Anoint the candle with a few drops of basil oil and place within your circle. Light your candle and breathe in the scent of the oil.

Hold the locket in your hand and meditate upon your experiences. Calmly think through what has happened, its causes and consequences, and ask yourself how it has changed your life. As you sit quietly meditating, repeat aloud the incantation.

Take a last pinch of marjoram and anoint it with some drops of basil. Place this inside your silver locket and carry it about on your person. In time, the meaning and reasoning behind everything will become clear.

By the power of
Universal thought

Open my mind to
a new life course

Glossary of Terms

Affirmation – the act of verbally or physically confirming ideas and thoughts. Affirmations can be written or spoken.

Anointment – to place oil on something or someone. Anointment is used in spell-casting to fuse candle heat with essential oils.

Bewitch – to entrance another person or animal with magical power.

Cleansing or clearing – the process of removing negative feelings and thoughts through magic ritual. Cleansing or clearing must take place before spell-casting can proceed.

Incantation – a passage, phrase or chant that is repeated aloud once or numerous times to invoke magic.

Love placket – a pocket of material made by the spell-caster into which objects and ingredients are placed to enhance a spell.

Meditation – the act of focusing the mind on calm, affirming thoughts. Meditation is used in spell-casting to visualise and affirm ones desires.

Ritual – a stylised and formalised physical or mental act performed when spell-casting.

Spell-casting – the ritualised act of magic. Spells are usually cast with the use of candles, oils, a magic wand and a sacred circle. The act of spell-casting relies upon meditation and visualisation, with affirmations or invocations repeated aloud.

Spell-sachet – a small bag of material made by the spell-caster into which magical objects and properties are placed. Spell-sachets can be made for the spell-caster or another person he or she seeks to help.

Talisman – a piece of jewellery or an object that carries magical power.

Waning moon – the phrase of the moon in decline. A waning moon will be seen in the early hours of the morning.

Waxing moon – the phrase of the moon in growth. A waxing moon can be seen in the early hours of the evening.